The Joys of Engrish

The Joys of Engrish

Steven Caires

MICHAEL JOSEPH
an imprint of
PENGUIN BOOKS

Published by the Penguin Group
Penguin Books Ltd, 80 Strand, London WC2R 0RL, England
Penguin Group (USA) Inc., 375 Hudson Street, New York, New York 10014, USA
Penguin Group (Canada), 90 Eglinton Avenue East, Suite 700, Toronto, Ontario, Canada M4P 2Y3
(a division of Pearson Penguin Canada Inc.)
Penguin Ireland, 25 St Stephen's Green, Dublin 2, Ireland (a division of Penguin Books Ltd)
Penguin Group (Australia), 250 Camberwell Road,
Camberwell, Victoria 3124, Australia (a division of Pearson Australia Group Pty Ltd)
Penguin Books India Pvt Ltd, 11 Community Centre,
Panchsheel Park, New Delhi – 110 017, India
Penguin Group (NZ), cnr Airborne and Rosedale Roads, Albany,
Auckland 1310, New Zealand (a division of Pearson New Zealand Ltd)
Penguin Books (South Africa) (Pty) Ltd, 24 Sturdee Avenue,
Rosebank 2196, Johannesburg, South Africa

Penguin Books Ltd, Registered Offices: 80 Strand, London WC2R 0RL, England

www.penguin.com

First published 2005

Printed and bound in Italy by Printer Trento Srl

A CIP catalogue record for this book is available from the British Library

ISBN 0-718-14845-2

To all of my Engrish friends – everyone, everywhore...

Like newly born drops of water

My favourite dreams and wilful life

I like you in the recent days

Very wonderfully and more pleasantly

Introduction

'Pleasure is born here. Unintentionally with individuality and nonchalantly with sensibility.'

Engrish. More than a word, it's a cultural phenomenon. And it's begun attracting attention across the English-speaking world. Surprising English phrases, ranging from the quaint to the profane, have long appeared in Japanese advertising and product design. They are apparently there only to make products and services look *cool* to the Japanese public; but observe what happens when we dig a little deeper: somehow, oddball truths seem to emerge. Irony, existentialism and dark humour appear where only fun-loving phraseology had been intended.

'I wonder why coffee tastes so good when you're naked with your family'

(on coffee package)

'I am always full of appetite. Then it is fine' (on bag of walnuts)

'Make your dream get bigger!' (on boxer short packaging)

We may never entirely understand the processes at hand, but it cannot be denied that Engrish can yield kernels of wisdom, beauty and profundity. Indeed, there exist moments of mysterious poetic wit and subtle nuance that transcend the art form.

It's no coincidence that the message boards at Engrish.com have attracted an intellectual crowd of native English speakers from around the globe. The fact that the message boards have retained a friendly, yet intellectually stimulating, atmosphere is a testament to the power of Engrish.

For those new to Engrish, I am confident you will come to share my own belief that something is here that can be appreciated on many levels and on multiple occasions.

So, when reading *The Joys of Engrish*, please make sure to enjoy your pleasant with vigour!

Steven Caires
creator of *Engrish.com*

Our clothes makes healthy
and sexy impression to us.
It transforms yourself
completely, and giving
you happy times.

NO.	3880	
SIZE	QUALITY	
Free	綿 50% アクリル 50%	
PRICE		

PRESEN BY **MISS EWE CO.,LTD.**
TOKYO JAPAN Tel 03-5486-

Love
cherry

Pleasant things...
I really love them!

BOスペンケース ラブチエリー
714円

HANG – O – BAR

GONNA BE HANGOVER

FREE DRINK ¥5000
DRAFT BEER
WHISKY
SPIRIT

6

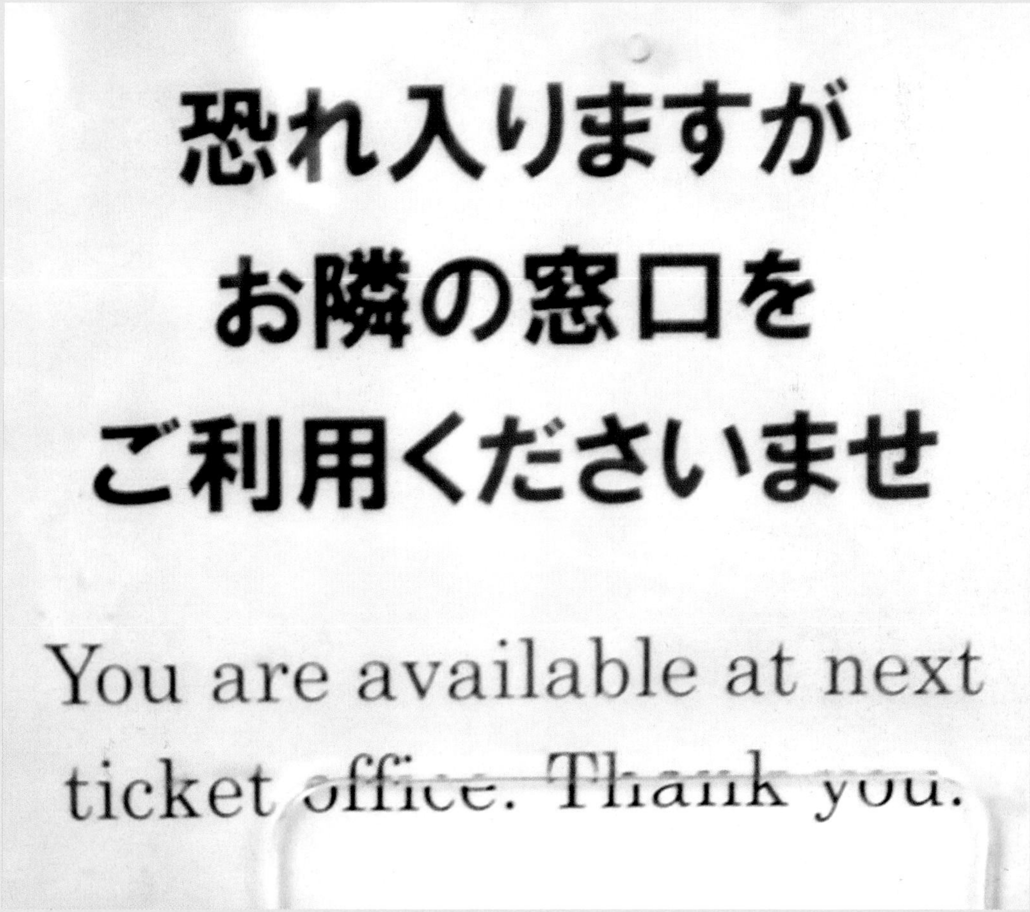

恐れ入りますが
お隣の窓口を
ご利用くださいませ

You are available at next
ticket office. Thank you.

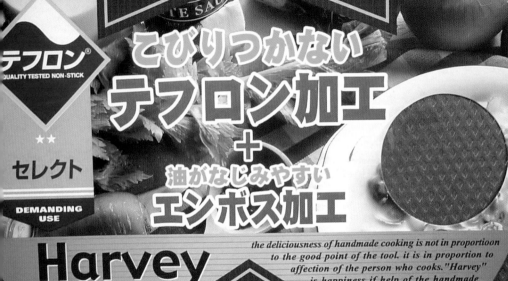

CHERRY BLACK

WELCOME TO PLEASURE WORLD.
GUARANTEED HIGH QUALITY.

LOS ANGELES CA.

THE SKY
AND A RIVER
ARE WIDE
it seems
that the sun
is wrong
BIG-SIZE

FOOD MARKET
ポテト
POTATO

Welcome friends
I am POTATO.

ベリー
ファッキング
英会話

Terreko's English Lesson～テリコ先生の英会話教室

VERY FUCKING ENGLISH LESSON

SUMMER / FALL 2001 COURSE SCHEDULE

UPLINK
FACTORY

150-0041
東京都渋谷区神南1-8-17
横山ビル5F
tel.03-5489-07██
fax.03-5489-07██

HOXY will always offer you a rich and comfortable life with paper.

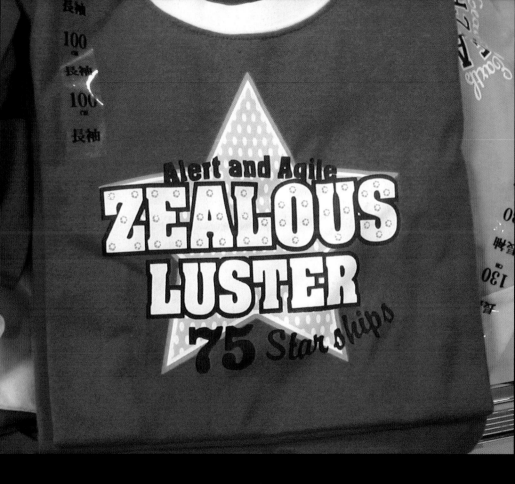

NATURAL TASTE

富士山のひかり

FUJISAN no HIKARI

Smell is rich, and they are the sweets
which used much chocolate of the strong
taste and which was made. Give a friend
your wonderful recollections that it
traveled this ground with this chocolate.

College Plus

for all sensuous people Line:A

Authentic necessaries for official
and personal life scene.

SHEETS:50

21

Berry pop life

Like newly born drops of water.
My favorite dreams and willful life.
I like you in the recent days.
Very wonderfully and more pleasantly.

price / menu

cut+shanpoo+blow	5,000
parm +cut+shanpoo+blow	10,000~
point parm +cut+shanpoo+blow	8,000
strate parm +cut+shanpoo+blow	12,000
color +cut+shanpoo+blow	10,000~
color +shanpoo+blow	7,500~
henna +cut+shanpoo+blow	11,000~
henna +shanpoo+blow	8,500~
shanpoo+blow	3,500
treatment	2,000~

clay esthe pack/sp etc...

MONKEY BROTHERS

HELP

MONKEY BROTHERS

© 1999 by R.U.P

This pleasant group is always
good company, and they
have superb fashion sense.

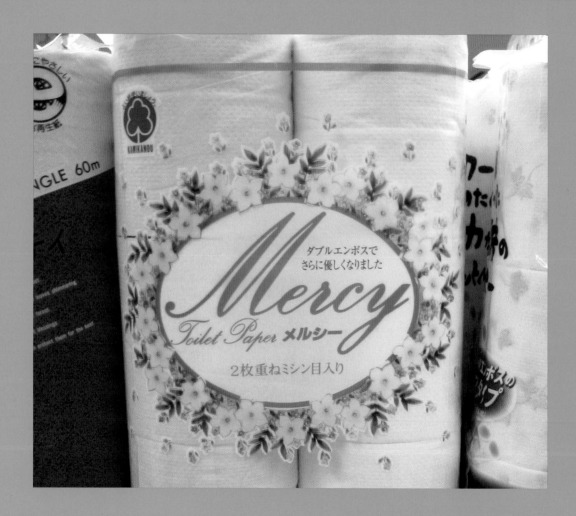

PRINCESS FLOWER
There are nice goods nearby.
Come hither, come hither, come hither!

32

ツインセット

Ravishing virgin®

HOTEL

H·O·T·E·L
·T·A·S·T·Y·

High Social Communication Hotel

HOTEL
·TA·S·T·Y·

i n

close

IT IS RECOMMENDED
JUST FOR
A FASHION
SENSITIVE PERSON
GOOD APPEARANCE
AND HIGH QUALITY
FIT TOGETHER.
PERFECT TO WEAR
MADE IN CHINA
MEDIUM

WiLLのコンセプトは「遊びゴコロと本物感」。
心に語りかけるデザインと
本質にこだわった機能をもつWiLLプロダクツ。
持っているだけでワクワクするような
ライフスタイルの新しい提案が、
WiLLには、いっぱい詰まっています。

LIFE PACKAGE

● ミニノートパソコンに
● 電子手帳に
● コンパクトCDプレーヤーに

ミニノートパソコン
サイズ

サイズ/約W255×H195mm

JOYFUL IMPRESSION
WE PRODUCE IT
FOR WHOLE HUMAN BEINGS

groing in the dark

a selection of gentlemen

The more free time I have, the more I tend to think of bad things
I want no more time competition
From now I need more leisurely time

NATURAL & HEALTHY

Mild and pleasant to the taste.
Please choose your favorite one for cheerful life.
Surely, It makes you happy.

CHOCO CAKES

As for beautiful harmony to play,
it is probably to reflect it elegantly
this chocolate cake
【 your tea time 】

チョコケーキ

Listen,
do you believe
when I say?

I touched a tiny nature. I tasted and enjoyed "nature"
This is extremely luxurious nature.
I am absorbed in nature. A naughty act of nature.

To live a day with nature ■■■■■■

で！ ジュージュー焼いて召し上

You can enjoy cocking "jyu-jyu" your meat by yourself, as you like.

レア！ ミディアム！ 思いのままに…

ジュージュー焼いて

Lemon SandCookies
レモンサンドクッキー

CocoaBanana SandCookies
ココアバナナサンドクッキー

SIZE M
WAIST 76-84cm

UNCONFORTABLY GUARANTEED
COMFORTABLY ABOUT GOOD QUALITY

BOXERS
products

SIZE LL
WAIST 94-104cm

KNIT BOXER

MEN'S KNIT BOXER BRIEF

UNCONFORTABLY GUARANTEED
IT'S COMFORTABLY ABOUT GOOD QUALITY

KNIT BOXERS
xinhe products

We think that we want to contribute to society through daiamond drilling and wire sawing.

CORE

Call 045-544-███

LILY BELL

It is living happily together wholly.
But it is also disagreeable to
become lonely although he
wants to come apart occasionally.

KEEP AIR CLEAN

WE ♥ SMOKING
This ashtray is for all tobacco lovers.
Let's enjoy smoking and keep manner.

Pied ◎ Beautyful

Glory be to God for dappled things-
For skies of couple-color as a brinded cow;

FLOWER COMMUNICATION

The flowers in recollection sing a poem in sepia color. Time seems to return to the turn of it's beautiful melody flow. Please listen to the dream a fresh heart discloses. Please look at my fresh face. Please receive it just when you open your heart. A bouquet to all of you over the world.

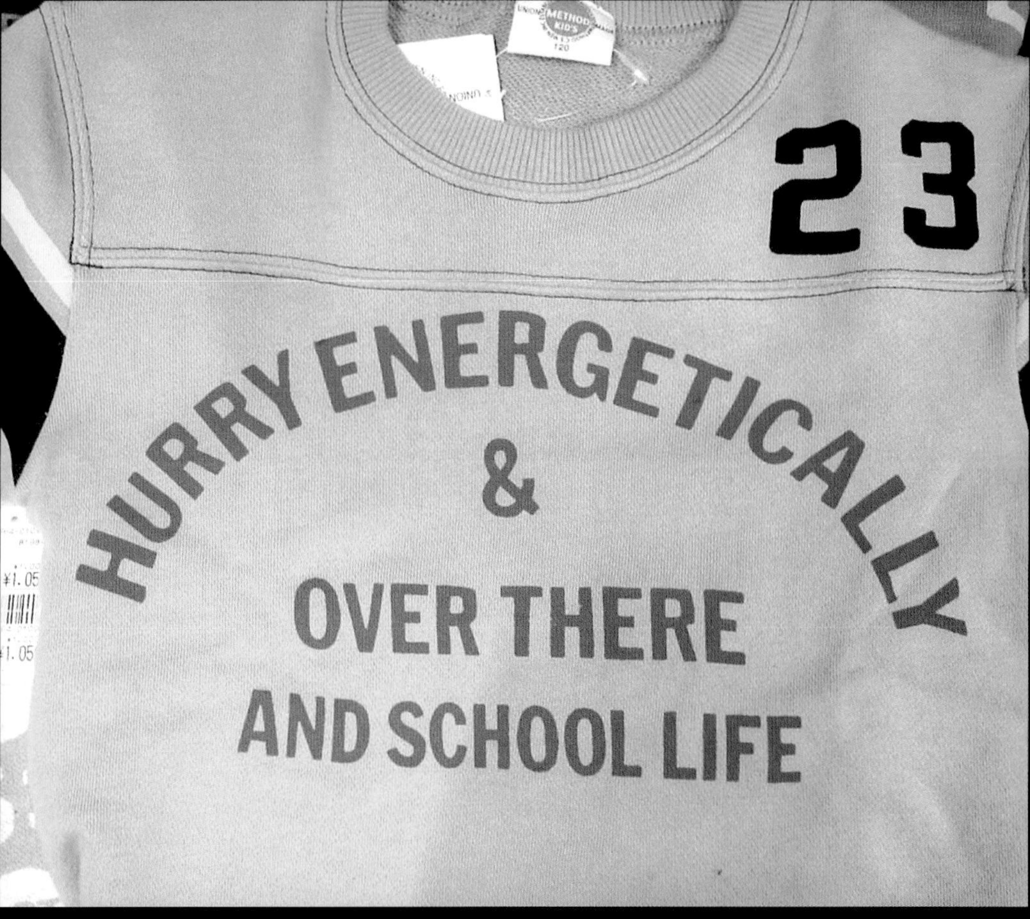

23

HURRY ENERGETICALLY
&
OVER THERE
AND SCHOOL LIFE

¥1.05

1.05

note
book

size 252mm x 179mm
30 sheets 6mm ruling

We wish that your life is
going to be fabulously enjoyable
with using this notebook.

subject

_____

name

_____

Let's go out in a poetry mood.

使用後は必ずこの釦を
押して下さい。

YOU LADY WILL PUSH
THIS BUTTON BEFORE
LEAVING.

OUTRAGEOUS BAY LEAF POWER

（ボタン付）
綿100% インドネシア製

（税込）
¥680
146　1375-0042

4 937354 037719

綿100%

吸汗速乾ゴム
使用

MB

TRUNKS COTTON 100%

MY BOY®

Make your dreamget bigger!

COMFORTER COVER

掛け HAPPY SLEEP
ぶとんカバー

You could sleep very comfortably.....

サイズ 45cm×90cm

PILLOW CASE
HAPPY SLEEP
ピロ
ケース

You could sleep
very comfortably....

Winning or losing is not a problem.
Enjoying is the most important matter.

300

Do you like bowling?
Let's play bowling.
Breaking down the pins
and get hot communication.

PERFECT KIDS

IN EVERY WAY

CERTAINLY PERTINENT AT THIS JUNCTURE

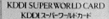

Time tells all.

Time is made by oneself. Gentle time is on my side.
Time spent in unease is now being converted
into time spent in serenity.

Curious Time

Time spent in unease is now being converted into time spent in serenity.
I depart with my full bag of time. Here is my own secret time.

81

I SAW
THE MOVIE
WHICH
COULD CRY
VERY MUCH!

Lavatory

It has separated
to the male
and the woman.
Don't mistake.

Lavatory

It has separated
to the male
and the woman.
Don't mistake.

DY-151 ₩ MATSUNO HOBBY

快適生活雑貨

TOILET BRUSH

We'll advise you about your 'stickiness' about your daily life.
To the people enjoying their life...

品質表示		
材質	(濾紙) ポリプロピレン	
	(柄) ポリプロピレン	
耐熱温度	90℃	

MATSUNO INDUSTRY CO.,LTD.
1-3-47 URIWARIMINAMI, HIRANO-KU, OSAKA

4 978929 441517

MADE IN CHINA

袋:PP ラベル

87

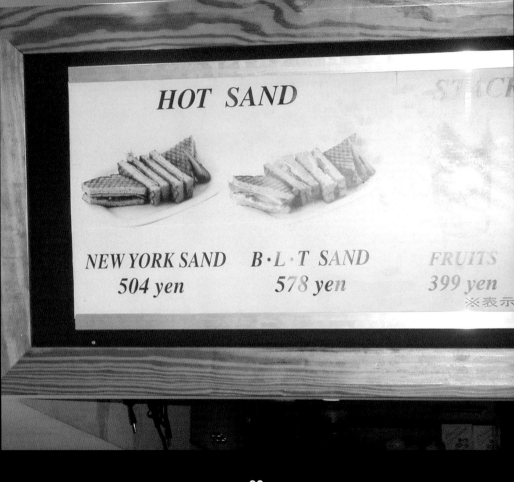

HOT SAND

STACK

NEW YORK SAND
504 yen

B·L·T SAND
578 yen

FRUITS
399 yen

※表示

手作りサンドイッチの店

SANDORE

Fresh Sandwich with our whole heart.

サ・ン・ド・ー・レ

楽しいパーテイに
サンドイッチをどうぞ。

5F A-TITTY 原宿・表参道店
Wedding & Party & Space

4F 株式会社　東京設備
株式会社　ラインヒル

3F LIVE STUDIO

CLOVER 🍀 STORY
I wish to sing a duet with
transparent time.

You'll have mind
forgive everythi

If you become angry
or nervous, hold communion
with nature.

Beard papa

pursues handmade,
freshness and deliciousness,
and particular about the material
and particular about the material
and addition thing such as
an antiseptic never uses for health

Very few people cannot know this by now,
however we are informing
you again to be sure.
Knowing this can change your world.

Another dream to you!

Mushroom

WORK LIKE MAGIC!

I am full of yearnings and dreams.

Nice Day!

They are absorbed in pleasure.

spend a day happily.

SCROLL

You would wait for such
car fragrance.

UNDER GROUND

SINCE 2001

Therefore I made it.
Car fragrance
which cool guy has.

PECOLO

100

We think that it will always be with smile.
Then, a pleasant thing comes.

CUBIC ANIMALS
They are very pleasant friends.

McKINLEY®

We made this specially for you.Man can't
exist without air and water and this bag.
We must trust to divine providence.

College

NOTEBOOK

*This is the most comfortable notebook
you have ever run into.*

●

30SHEETS

TITLE

視機能検査

メガネ/コンタクト

三邦堂

1 F

NEW SMOKERS!
JOIN THE FUN

GREAT TABACCONIST

喫煙具専門

kagaya

1 F

Toilet Seat Cover

O-TYPE

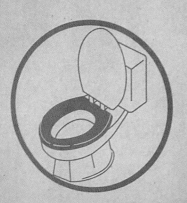

Natural material: Its color and texture make a room of peace... Its warmth and gentleness relieve one's mind... Its simplicity and naivete never lose one's interest... Our lives and culture were made from and were developed by natural materials. In busy, everyday life, people of today have less chance to touch nature. Flower, nuts, ocean, twig, rock, leaf, wind, sky, sand, tree, water, river, forest, soil, plant and the Earth... The blessings of nature are the blessings of people. Take a pause, have a rest. Then, look back yourself and reconsider your life.

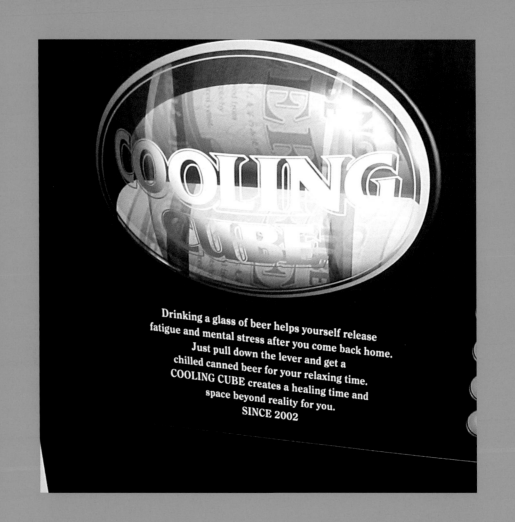

Drinking a glass of beer helps yourself release
fatigue and mental stress after you come back home.
Just pull down the lever and get a
chilled canned beer for your relaxing time.
COOLING CUBE creates a healing time and
space beyond reality for you.
SINCE 2002

衝突注意

Clash

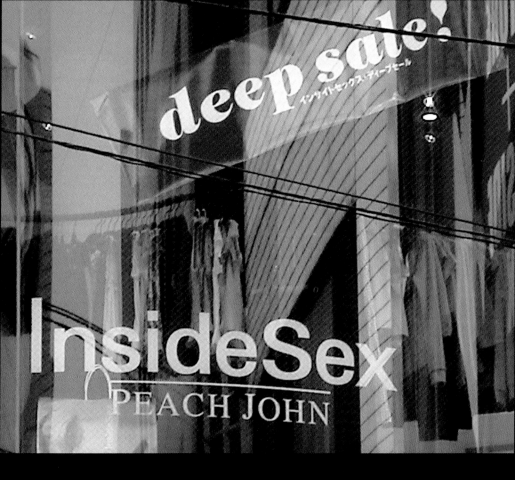

とべる 豆乳 とうにゅう

大豆イソフラボンでイキイキ

黒胡麻きなこ

栄養補助食品

This is the health food built with the soybean.
If it puts into soup, a drink, etc., it can eat stil more deliciously
Everybody, a family, will be continued every day.

粉　末

NET 120g

ECOLOGY
of the elephant

Huge body,Long nose, big ear, and tucks
are the elephant's chalacteristic.

BIOLOGY
cram cream

puti
fresh
© LUBE SHEEP 2003

Happy fruits is very delicious.
I will eat this and will become
fortunate all together!

HALOGEN LIGHT

MULTI PROTECTION

 防滴タイプ

白光色・長寿命

伸縮自在 3段式スタンド
高さ調整
無段階96cm〜185cm

 **500W**

This is "The light!!." This products is called "Halogen light." The reason why it is "The light" is that that products can be very active in a variety of scene such as a site of construction, work in the garage, party and something like that. This lighat stand vertically. The hight can be changed from 96cm to 185cm. Also, the head can be turned at any angle in horizontally and moved in about angle of 45 degree vertically. This is "The light" because of these reasons.

96cm
〜
185cm

● 用途・場所に応じ
高さが簡単に調整

1灯
三脚式

AKS-500
ハロゲン投光器500W

輸入販売元
県央貿易（株）

4941901070524

 紙
箱

プラ
中の袋

当店は初期不良以外の商品の返品交換には応じていません。商品を
よくご確認の上お買い上げ下さい。

なお初期不良の交換にはレシートが必要になります。レシートが無い
場合は対応致しかねますのでレシートは必ずお受け取り下さい。

また各階清算になっております。他フロアへの商品の持ち出しはご遠
慮下さい。

To a visitor

Our shop is not a duty-free shop.
It has not responded to returned-goods exchange of unexpected goods faulty
the first stage.
Please purchase goods after affirmation well.
Moreover, it is each story liquidation. Carrying out of the goods to other floors
and carrying in should withhold.

•pastor's belief•

Confession

(for the best) teacher.

Experience is good

preach

•DESPAIR GIVES COURAGE TO A COWARD•

DEEDS, NOT WORDS.

110
110
110
110

化粧室は後方へ
For Restrooms,
Go back toward your behind.

14 ↑

白身魚と貝柱のグリル 彩り野菜のクリーム
Today's fresh fish and scallop grill

モッツァレラチーズを包んだ牛肉のパン粉
Beef cut-let with mozallera cheese

Formagge=Cheese

カマンベール
Camembert

ブリアサヴァラン
Brillat savarin

ロックフォール
Roguefart

レビノスモーク ……
Reybino

4種盛り合わせ …………………………
Assorted Cheese

CLEAN!

Keep Clean Environment with taking to Everyone's heart.
Produced by Teramoto corporation

TERAMOTO

TITTY BOO
TOWER

7F TITTYBOO PARTY ROOM
6F TITTYBOO PARTY ROOM
5F TITTYBOO PARTY ROOM
4F TITTYBOO PARTY ROOM
3F TITTYBOO PARTY ROOM
2F TITTYBOO WEDDING DRESS
1F TITTYBOO RECEPTION ROOM
B1 TITTYBOO MACHINE ROOM
B2 TITTYBOO PARTY ROOM

TEL 03-5464-19■■

株式会社ティティー■■カンパニー

This is a rerax space.

please make y...e.

BiS-Ⅱ

...store where slot are pleasant and exciting.

Land mean

Future voices
need to be
heard
eyebrows
are always.

若鶏の細切り肉

包丁入らず。煮物、焼物、炒め物に

Shicken

若どりもも肉

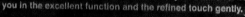

遠赤外線セラミックによる暖かさが
体の芯まで温もりを伝えます。

中国高級綿

新疆ウイグル綿

しなやかな風合いやさしい肌ざわり綿100

"UIGURU COTTON" which the higt Chinese class cotton
which pinched the hand that it was selected carefully was used for 100% wraps
you in the excellent function and the refined touch gently.

84-94

Beautiful color

The sky is

beautiful today, isn't it?

We're having

a spell of mind weather.

PHOTO PRINT

TOILET TISSUE

カラー花束 ®

HANATABA is a colored tissue paper taking advantage
of the regenerated paper having affection for
the earth. Its refreshing fragrance sends you a confortable time.

BABY
SHOOT

●ベビーシュート

車内用
ゴミ入れや、
小物整理に!

■使用方法
シートのヘッドレストに取りつけるか、フック等で吊り下げてください。

CAR LIFE SUPPORT

CAPSULE CHILDREN

Very wonderfully and more pleasantly.

SURFER BOY MET
A PENGUIN WITH
ITS BABY
THEN, SURFING WAS
DONE WITH THREE PEOPLE
FOR ONE DAY INSIDE,
AND IT ENJOYED
FULLNESS FULLY.
A PROMISE   WAS EVADED
WITH   LET'S PLAY
ABSOLUTELY   AGAIN,
AND IT   SAID
PIXY-CAL

The life in the world of value of existence is done.

The point of view of the thing which was different from the general person and the way of thinking.

The graphics of the assertion.

150

HEARTY
COLLECTION

We cheer everybody who communications
with all the heart.
That's the reason why our products are alive.

produced by Santamonica

ウエットティシュ

MYWET

COOL & REFRESHING TISSUE FOR NEW LIFE

OPEN

by SANSHOSHIGYO Co.,Ltd.

Feeling
Clover

**Life is always taking care of
me; I will recompense it before long.**

**This vital life will remain
the object of my gentle care.**

Gitly ♥ Cherry
Nurtured with care,
and there it blooms.

G-HOUSE
HAMMOCK SUPPORTER
First-rate clothes made for you by top-notch merchandising staff.
ハンモック
サポーター
これは、商品の裏側の写真です。
やさしいフィット感の立体サポーター
開発特許商品
特許第3148833号
053660
310
¥800
M
グレー
0720-00 5745202A

The child was thrown into ecstasies over his new toy.

★ ★ ★ ★ ★

Chain Gang

His pistol went off accidentally.

His pistol went off accidentally.
The child was thrown into ecstasies over his new toy.

3

★ ★ ★ ★ ★

His pistol went off accident...

I wonder why coffee tastes so good when your'e naked with your family.

They are ideal for your relaxation, children's snacks, and to take with you on your day out. Their cute size and rich flavor will bring happiness to your pockets.

生クリーム10%入

生クリームクッキー
プチスイート

Elephanto with sweet flower

All around us,
our own world of wonder!
Can't you see how chic we are?

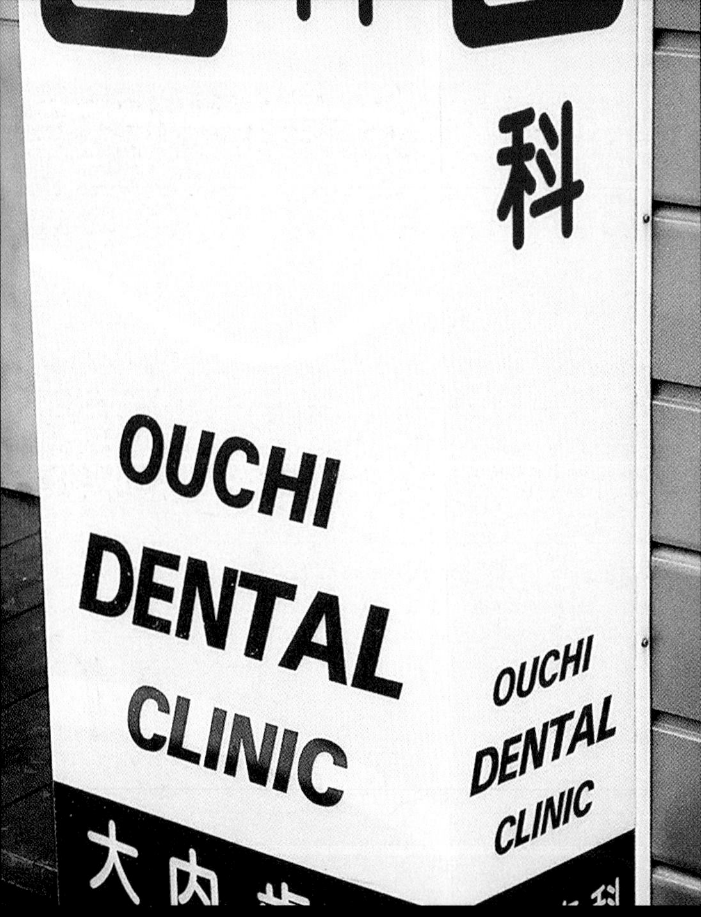

科

OUCHI
DENTAL
CLINIC

OUCHI
DENTAL
CLINIC

大内歯

I'm boring...

Kuroro

He is a black cat and a name is KURORO. Since he is lonely, he wants a friend.

Vesper!

I feels shy and there is
nothing something!

©BERRYBERRY

CALENDAR 2005

当店での両替はご遠慮願います。
Sorry. We can not change.

m glad to know
you're fine.

That is about all I want to tell you this time.

The highest goods are offered at a cheap price.
Good goods will surely be found.

cherry tomato

A cherry tomato is very sweet. and juicy.
It is very good also for health.

It is fruitiy even if it takes.

Love cherry

Pleasant things...
I really love them!

I'm in a very fine mood.
All are new. Anticipation of
a wonderful encounter!!

198202

Hopes are at my side.

My dream that
has begun to
move.

Swarms
of winter gnats
are still around

yand the gentle

warbling and

chattering

Pleasure is born here.

unintentionally with individuality and
nonchalantly with sensibility

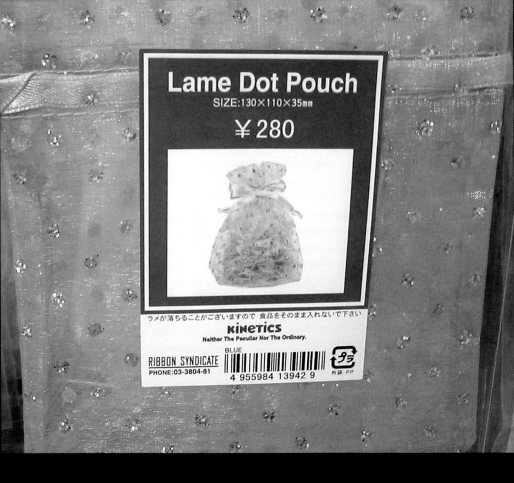

185

TOUGHBOX WIDE

The TOUGH BOX helps your life in the way.

You can arrenge various things by using TOUGH BOX.
For example,video-cassettes,CDs,MDs,drugs,tools etc...
Any thng you like can be packed in the TOUGH BOX.

VIDEO CD MD DRAG TOOL

DANGER

BIOHAZARD

IT SUPPOSED TO HELP
ALL THE PEOPLE
IT SUPPOSED
TO MAKE THEM HAPPY
BUT WE GOT
TO RECOGNIZE IT DANGER

You fond a treasure at last.
I have only a faint memory of that affair.
The scene still comes to mind now and then.
I have a vividly remember
seeing you here.

Bravo!

インターホン

Interphone

ご用のお客様は、インターホンで
係員におたずね下さい。

When you have something to do
please call the operation staff
by interphone.

The Alligators

There so many alligators,
so many dreams.
All are grittering, aren't they?

do
do

FELT
ROOM SHOES

USE

When you feeling chilly

such as in the kitchen,
in the living room,
and in the bed room.

SIZE

FREE

COMPOSITION

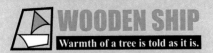

WOODEN SHIP

Warmth of a tree is told as it is.

The pleasant tale which the wooden small world unfolds.

WOODEN SHIP

To favorite you of wooden goods

WOOD&PECKER

ーキと デザート *Cake & Dessert*

ケーキ各種 ─────────── Cake 450

ケーキトレイをお持ち致しますので、お選び下さい。
Please choose from ass or cake dessert Tray

ケーキ セット コーヒーor紅茶 +750
Cake Set(Caffee or tea)

My Favorite Taste

肉詰れんこんフライ

~ *Nikuzume Renkon* ~

We reproduced the old-fashioned OKAZU. Severely selected materials are processed by the traditional method of production. Please enjoy having the real OKAZU at dinner or lunchtime.

明治ケンコーハム

The small pigs which carry happiness
convey a feeling to everybody.
Therefore, it will make a living happily.

MEN'S
SOCKS

Pleasing style

サイズ 25-27cm

Casual Socks
for MEN
with embroidery

size 25-27cm

T STYLE

ズ 25～27cm

GRASSFIELD

in its place.A place for everything, and everything

100% ALL YOUR STRENGTH
Pratact it by that HAND.
HEAD WEEDS
It is a foolish bird that soils its own nest.

Snatch nation

Let's walk to
the next town in the night

Picture Credits

All photos supplied by the author unless otherwise stated.

1. Baby sweater
2. Clothing label (courtesy of Anders & Noriko Olsson)
3. Pencil case/small bag
4. Shopping centre (courtesy of Paul Thomas)
5. Hotel (courtesy of Steve Bryant)
6. Business sign for bar (courtesy of Jeremyah Corner)
7. Closed counter sign (courtesy of Fahruz)
8. Teflon frying pan (courtesy of Fahruz)
9. Storage boxes
10. T-shirt
11. T-shirt
12. Fruit and vegetable market (courtesy of Matthew Webster)
13. Hairdresser's
14. Vending machine for canned drinks (courtesy of Michael Chludenski)
15. Cake mix
16. Parking station
17. Schedule for an English course (courtesy of Mark Schreiber)
18. Stationery
19. T-shirt
20. Cookies (courtesy of Fahruz)
21. Stationery
22. Sweatshirt
23. Rates sign for hairdresser's
24. Pencil case
25. Rates sign for hairdresser's
26. Pharmacy (courtesy of Charles Rich)
27. Money tin
28. Boxer shorts
29. Store carrier bag (courtesy of Richard Jew)
30. Toilet paper
31. Hot water dispenser
32. Stuffed toy (courtesy of Ash)
33. Clothing brand label
34. Hotel (courtesy of Michael Degelbeck)
35. T-shirt
36. Clothing label

About the Author

Steven Caires, founder of Engrish.com, started to collect Engrish items back in 1987 when he first went to Japan as a student. Over the course of ten years living in Tokyo as both a student and a 'salaryman', he would frequently bring Engrish candy, gum and other small items back with him to the US as gifts for friends. In 1996, when the worldwide web was just starting to become mainstream, the thought of compiling 'Engrish' in a website was a natural extension of his collection and Engrish.com was born.

Engrish.com now attracts more than 8 million new visitors a year.

www.engrish.com